CIGAR
Aficionado's
POCKET GUIDE

M. SHANKEN COMMUNICATIONS, INC.
NEW YORK

Printed in China

9   8   7   6   5   4   3   2   1
Digit on the right indicates the number of this printing

ISBN 1-881659-45-3

Cover and interior design by Ellen Diamant and Claudia Marulanda
Research and editing assistance by Ann Berkhausen and Amy Lyons

For subscriptions to *Cigar Aficionado*, please call: (800) 922-2442 or write:
M. Shanken Communications, Inc.
387 Park Avenue South
New York, NY 10016

Visit our website at: http://www.cigaraficionado.com

Distributed by Running Press Book Publishers
125 South Twenty-second Street
Philadelphia, PA 19103-4399

PREFACE

Since the first edition of this little guide was published a few years ago, the cigar renaissance has mushroomed beyond even my wildest expectations.

In the surge of antismoking fervor that began in the 1970s, cigar smokers suffered harassment and inconvenience far beyond reason. Restrictions sprang up everywhere: "Smoking Section. No pipes or cigars allowed" was common on menus and restaurant walls. By the early 1990's, the remaining devotees of premium hand-rolled cigars were condemned to second-class citizenship.

With the launch of CIGAR AFICIONADO in 1992, everything changed. The small coterie of passionate cigar lovers suddenly had a voice, a forum to express the truth about its favorite pastime: that cigars are one of life's truly great pleasures. At the same time, cigar makers began to respond to the demand for full-flavored, rich-tasting cigars. Tobacconists introduced new and improved products. Attracted by the lure of sophisticated pleasure, new smokers—especially young men in their late 20s and 30s, and some women, too—joined the fun. Celebrities who had hidden their enjoyment of cigars stepped forward to publicly announce that they, too, loved a great smoke.

The change has been astonishing. As a visible symbol of a cultural shift, cigars have become the focus of national media attention. Cigar retailers are flourishing. Cigar makers can't make enough cigars to satisfy demand. Cigar dinners, cigar events, cigar clubs, even cigar-oriented restaurants abound.

The cigar is back. Enjoy it.

Marvin R. Shanken
Editor & Publisher, *Cigar Aficionado*

CONTENTS

5

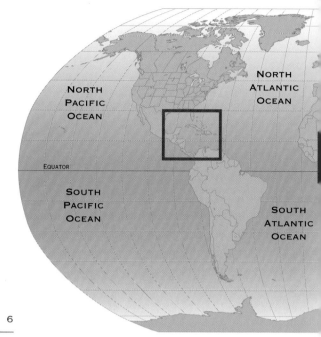

The Western world first learned of tobacco shortly after Christopher Columbus dropped anchor off the Cuban coast in October, 1492. Two of the men he sent ashore reported back that they had seen natives with "smoking heads." Columbus brought tobacco seeds back to Europe, and within eighty years this New World plant was in widespread use throughout the Old World.

It's fitting that Cuban tobacco was the first to be exported, for even now the Cuban product is considered by many—particularly lovers of hand-rolled, premium cigars—to be the finest available. Today tobacco is grown in many parts of the world, with the dark tobacco used in quality cigars found mainly in three tropical areas: Latin America and the Caribbean; near the South China Sea in East Asia; and West Africa.

Because tobacco is genetically stable—that is, the seeds of tobacco plants remain genetically pure from one generation to the next—you might expect that Cuban-seed tobacco grown in the Dominican Republic would taste identical to that grown from the

CIGAR TOBACCO

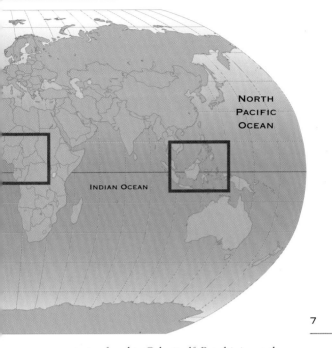

NORTH
PACIFIC
OCEAN

INDIAN OCEAN

same strain of seed in Cuba itself. But this is not the case. Like wine grapes, tobacco plants are affected by variations in soil and climate. These variations can produce differences—striking or subtle—in the taste of the final product.

CUBA

Perhaps the best tobacco-growing region in the world is the Vuelta Abajo, which comprises most of Pinar del Rio, the westernmost province of Cuba. About 100,000 acres of the rich, red soil here are planted with cigar tobacco, but the best of all comes from a small area near the towns of San Juan y Martinez and San Luis. Plantations well-known for their wrapper leaves include Laguira and El Corojo ("The Wrapper"), while Hoyo de Monterrey specializes in filler tobacco.

Small *vegas* (plantations) of up to 150 acres are privately owned, while larger ones belong to the government. Each plantation's tobacco is sold at fixed prices to one or more of the government-run cigar factories in Havana; each factory, in turn, may produce several brands, either for export or for domestic consumption.

Several other areas of Cuba are devoted to tobacco cultivation as well. The Semi-Vuelta, also in Pinar del Rio, specializes in filler tobacco; so does Remedios, in the central part of the island, whose product is used mainly for blending. The tobacco grown in Oriente, in the southeast, is of somewhat lesser quality, and is used in cigars destined for the local market.

Probably the best tobacco region after the Vuelta Abajo is Partido, just southwest of Havana. Traditionally, Partido specialized in the green wrapper leaves known as candela; now that green cigars are out of favor on the world market, the area is experimenting, quite successfully, with Connecticut-seed wrappers.

DOMINICAN REPUBLIC

When the United States embargoed all Cuban products in 1962, following Fidel Castro's revolution, the largest market for Havanas suddenly evaporated. Cigar manufacturing firms—some of them American-owned—began to look elsewhere for land that could produce fine tobacco. They found it in Cuba's Caribbean neighbor, the Dominican Republic.

This island nation is now the world's largest producer of handmade premium cigars, and its output continues to grow. More than 18,000 acres of tobacco were planted for the 1996 crop, 50 percent more than the previous year. Several types of filler tobacco are grown here; *piloto Cubano*, for example, whose seed originated in Cuba's Vuelta Abajo, is noted for its richness and intensity, while *olor* has a more neutral flavor. The types are mixed together in varying proportions to produce distinctive blends.

The best tobacco-growing region of the Dominican Republic is the six-mile-wide Yaque Valley, which extends from the city of Santiago (in the north central part of the country) about 25 miles northwest to the town of Esperanza. Approximately 4500 tiny tobacco farms dot the area. Some farmers have contracts with specific manufacturers, but most sell to middlemen called *empacadores* (packers), who process the tobacco before selling it to cigar producers.

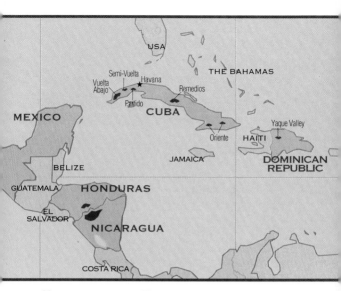

HONDURAS AND NICARAGUA

These two Central American nations share a
common border—and a common history of
troubled tobacco industries in the 1980s.

In Honduras, the problem was disease. Honduran
cigar tobacco is almost exclusively Cuban-seed in
origin, a fact that the country's cigar makers point to
proudly when claiming that their product tastes more
like a true Havana than any other in the world. But
Cuban-seed tobacco is especially subject to infestations
of blue mold, which can destroy a tobacco field
virtually overnight. In the mid-1980s, when the
plague was at its height, the reputation of Honduras'
famously strong, rich-tasting cigars suffered as some
were made with inferior tobacco. But growers have
since found new ways to battle the mold, and the
industry is on the rebound.

Nicaragua's cigar industry is centered around the
towns of Jalapa and Estelí in the northwestern part
of the country near the Honduran border. And in the
1980s, geography was destiny: it was precisely this area
that was the scene of the heaviest fighting between
Sandinista government forces and the U.S.-backed
Contras throughout the country's 10-year-long civil
war. Tobacco fields were mined, and curing barns were
used as military barracks by both sides. The industry

suffered major setbacks, but since the mid-1990s it has come roaring back; in fact, in 1996 Nicaragua leapt ahead of Jamaica and Mexico to become the third largest exporter of cigars to the United States (after the Dominican Republic and Honduras).

MEXICO

The state of Veracruz, on the southern curve of Mexico's Gulf coast, is home to this country's two tobacco-growing regions. Filler tobacco and a native black *tabaco negro* used for maduro wrappers grow in the northern part of the state. Maduro wrappers are grown in the south as well, specifically in the San Andres Valley, but here the specialty is a strain of Sumatra-seed tobacco used in both binders and wrappers. The Sumatra-seed wrapper leaves are prized for their silkiness and delicate vein structure.

ECUADOR

This South American country is best known for its high-quality wrapper leaves, both shade- and sun-grown. Both Sumatra-seed and Connecticut-seed varieties are used to produce wrappers that are silky to the touch and have great visual appeal as well, due to their excellent colors and very light vein structure.

BRAZIL

Most Brazilian cigar tobacco is of the local Mata Fina variety, which grows in the Bahia region on the central east coast. Frequently used as filler in premium cigars, Mata Fina is a dark, richly flavored tobacco with a touch of sweetness. The other native Brazilian tobacco, Arapiraca, comes from Alagoas, just north of Bahia. It is not widely used today, because of its lack of distinctive flavor.

CONNECTICUT

This New England state is the major exception to
the rule that premium cigar tobacco grows only in
tropical areas. The Connecticut River Valley north
of Hartford produces one of the finest wrappers in
the world: Connecticut Shade. The golden tan,
finely textured leaves have a high degree of elasticity
and a mild- to medium-bodied taste. Another type
grown here, Connecticut Broadleaf, is a sun-grown
tobacco used mainly for dark maduro wrappers; it is
thicker and more heavily veined than shade-grown.

CAMEROON/CENTRAL AFRICAN REPUBLIC

A high-quality, Sumatra-seed leaf known as Cameroon
wrapper is grown in both of these West African
nations. Greenish-brown to dark brown in color,
Cameroon leaf has a unique grain called "tooth"; it is
prized for its pleasant yet neutral flavor characteristics,
which make it an ideal wrapper for full-flavored
tobaccos. Management difficulties and bad weather
have led to decreased production in recent years.

INDONESIA AND THE PHILIPPINES

The archipelago of Indonesia is the source of the
wrapper leaf known as Sumatra-seed (or Java-seed),
which is now grown in a number of places around
the world. Actual Sumatra-grown wrapper tobacco is
usually dark brown in color and neutral in flavor; the
majority is used in the manufacture of small cigars.
The Philippines, Indonesia's neighbor to the northeast,
produces a hybrid strain of cigar tobacco that is mild
in flavor but very aromatic.

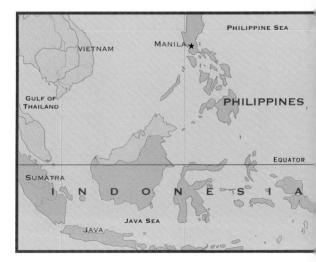

CIGAR MANUFACTURING

Making a hand-rolled cigar is a complicated art. Experienced farmers, master blenders and skilled rollers are essential to the process, and they carry out the time-honored tradition of producing premium cigars with great pride.

GROWING TOBACCO

The cigar-making process begins in the tobacco fields. The varieties of tobacco that are used for cigar production—Connecticut-seed or Cuban-seed, for example—provide varying flavors and leaf sizes.

It takes anywhere from 80-90 days for a seed to develop into a full-grown plant that is ready for harvest.

A worker inspects newly harvested tobacco leaves.

But in the field, tobacco is treated almost identically with one key distinction: whether it is sun- or shade-grown. Sun-grown tobacco is exposed to the full strength of the sun throughout the growing season. This makes for a more robust leaf with stronger flavors and darker colors. Shade-grown, normally reserved for wrapper leaves, is planted under a gauze-like tarp producing a more visually appealing, larger, thinner leaf with smaller veins.

The growing cycle is virtually identical for all cigar tobacco varieties. The seeds, the size of grains of sand, are germinated in a greenhouse and planted in raised seedbeds. It takes approximately six weeks for the plants to reach a height of six to eight inches. The strongest, healthiest plants with the most solid root structure are transplanted to the fields. Approximately 40 days after transplanting, the top part of the stalk is cut off. At 45 to 55 days, the first leaves, which practically lay on the ground, are removed and discarded. At the same time, the next row of leaves up—the leaves grow in concentric circles in groups of three up the stalk of the plant—is harvested; this is called the first priming (see photo page 14).

- The first priming yields the lightest and sweetest of the plants' leaves, which are used for binder and some wrapper. They are known for their combustion qualities because they are so thin and papery.

- The second priming is harvested approximately seven days after the first priming. It also has a sweet quality but has more nicotine in it, which makes it stronger and more flavorful. A higher percentage of this priming is used for wrapper, but it is still primarily used for binders and fillers.

- The third priming is considered the most elegant leaves on the plant, and up to 70 percent of them will be used for wrapper. They also have some sweetness and still higher percentages of nicotine, and are used to balance out filler blends.

TOBACCO PLANT
APPROXIMATELY 5-7 FEET HIGH

Topped Portion

PRIMINGS

6th

5th

4th

3rd

2nd

1st

The tobacco leaves are tied together in bunches, then hung to dry before beginning the fermentation process.

• The fourth priming has much more body, due to more exposure to sunlight. The leaves from this level of the plant are richer and usually darker in color. While this tobacco begins to be heavier in texture, it is also used for wrapper.

• The fifth priming includes one of the most robust leaves on the plant, especially in the Cuban-seed variety. In general, less wrapper comes from this priming; most of it is used for binder and filler. But if you see a very dark-wrapped cigar that is not a maduro, it may very well come from the fifth priming. By now, the leaf requires extended fermentation and processing to lighten its texture and reduce its strength if it is to be used for a wrapper. Given their thicker texture, these leaves also don't burn as well.

• The sixth priming is usually used only for long filler. It has the heaviest texture and is slow-burning. But it is very flavorful. Some companies age sixth priming tobacco as much as five years before putting it into cigars. It is not suitable for wrappers because the leaves get smaller near the top of the plant.

After the plant has reached maturity it is ready to be harvested. The exact timing for the harvesting depends on the weather and the farmer's experience

JAMES SUCKLING

The leaves dry in large wooden barns called casas de tabacos.

in judging the ripeness of the tobacco. Seed variety is also a factor, as some seed varieties grow more quickly then others; it takes anywhere from 80 to 90 days for a seed to develop into a full-grown plant.

After being harvested, the cigar tobacco enters the fermentation stage. In this stage the tobacco is slightly moistened, then piled in huge bales or stacks; temperatures inside the bales reach as high as 140°F as the tobacco "sweats" during the early stages of the fermentation. Some tobacco may be "turned" up to three or four times and remoistened before fermentation finally ceases. The process releases ammonia from the tobacco and reduces overall nicotine content.

The fermented tobacco is then wrapped in bales— usually surrounded by burlap—to age. Standard aging time is 18 months to two years, although some manufacturers keep inventories of tobacco as old as 10 years. The tobacco is then slightly dampened again to make it supple before being turned over to the rollers.

MAKING THE CIGAR

A cigar blend is created by a master blender, someone who combines tobaccos of varying tastes and strengths to create a balanced, harmonious smoke. Depending on its ring gauge, a cigar will contain a blend of between two and four different tobaccos. Each type of tobacco leaf is placed in different boxes at the roller's desk, and the roller is given the formula for the specific cigar he or she is making.

The roller takes the leaves and presses them together in his hand; he then places the leaves on a binder leaf—a flat, somewhat elastic leaf of tobacco—to hold it together. He rolls them together into a "bunch," cuts them to the appropriate length and then places them in the bottom half of a wooden mold. After he puts the upper half of the mold in place, he puts the entire box into a screw press. The press operator will usually break down the press once, turn the bunch inside the mold and then rebox and press the bunch again, for a total pressing time of about an hour.

17

BILL GENTILE

The cigar rollers follow a formula created by a master blender when crafting each cigar.

A torcedor, or cigar roller, inspects her newly rolled cigars for any defects before selecting cigars for a box.

Once the worker has pressed the cigar, he returns the wooden molds to the rolling tables. The roller removes the bunch and wraps it with the wrapper leaf, a supple, very elastic and visually beautiful leaf that has been cut in half. Keeping constant pressure on the bunch and the wrapper, the cigar maker rolls the leaf around the bunch and applies a bit of vegetable glue to bond the wrapper leaf together at the head so the cigar won't unravel.

Supervisors inspect each cigar by hand. They feel it for weight and for any hard spots, which could indicate a plug, or soft spots, which can cause an uneven burn. They reject defective cigars. Then, in most factories, workers weigh the cigars in bunches of 50. Good cigar makers will have less than 1 gram of variation between 50-cigar bunches. Bunches with significant weight variations may be returned to the roller.

AGING THE CIGAR

The next stop for cigars is the aging room. Most factories age their cigars a least 21 days, and some leave them in the aging room for anywhere from 90 to 180 days. This allows the different cigar tobaccos to "marry" and create a more balanced smoke. After aging, the cigars are selected for each box, checked for fine gradations in wrapper leaf color, and finally, packed in boxes for shipping.

Cigar box size varies, but typically a box holds 25 or 50 cigars.

After packaging, the cigars are aged again—for anywhere from 3 weeks to 6 months—before shipping.

SIZES & SHAPES

Cigar sizes have two dimensions: length (in either inches or centimeters) and ring gauge, a measurement divided into 64ths of an inch (or, in the European method, millimeters). A cigar with a ring gauge of 40, for example, measures 40/64th of an inch in diameter.

Cigar shapes are divided into two categories: *parejos*, which are the familiar cigars with straight sides, a closed head (the end you smoke), and an open foot (the end you light); and *figurados*, which include all irregularly-shaped cigars.

Please note that names for specific sizes and shapes are *not* standardized from brand to brand. The dimensions listed below represent an average or typical example of each format.

PAREJOS (STRAIGHT-SIDED CIGARS)

CHURCHILL: A large corona format. The traditional dimension is 7 inches by a 48 ring.

Churchill

Corona

Corona Gorda

Double Corona

CORONA: The traditional proportion is 5 1/2 to 6 inches with a ring gauge of 42 to 44.

CORONA GORDA: This long robusto format could be called a robusto extra, although its popularity preceded that of robustos. The traditional measurements are 5 5/8 inches by a 46 ring.

DOUBLE CORONA: The standard dimension is 7 1/2 to 8 inches by a 49 to 52 ring.

LONSDALE: The classic size is 6 1/4 inches by a 42 to 44 ring.

PANATELA: More popular in years past than today. This thin format varies more widely in length than almost any other cigar size, from 5 to 7 1/2 inches and from a 34 to 38 ring gauge.

PETIT CORONA: This short corona is usually 4 1/2 inches by a 40 to 42 ring gauge.

ROBUSTO: This short Churchill format is growing in popularity. The traditional size is 5 to 5 1/2 inches by a 50 ring gauge.

Lonsdale

Panatela

Petit Corona

Robusto

FIGURADOS

BELICOSO: Traditionally, a belicoso was a short pyramid, 5 or 5 1/2 inches in length with a shorter, more rounded taper at the head and a ring gauge generally of 50 or less. Today, belicosos are frequently coronas or coronas gordas with a tapered head.

CULEBRA: This most exotic shape is actually three panatelas braided together and banded as one cigar. You smoke them separately. They are usually 5 to 6 inches in length, most often with a 38 ring gauge. Culebras are hard to come by today.

DIADEMAS: A true torpedo. The head and foot on this cigar are both closed. It is usually 8 inches or longer and is often boxed individually. It has a ring gauge of 40 at the head and 52 to 54, or even larger, at the foot.

PERFECTO: This cigar is closed at both ends. The head is rounded, not tapered. The foot is closed like a torpedo or a diademas. It

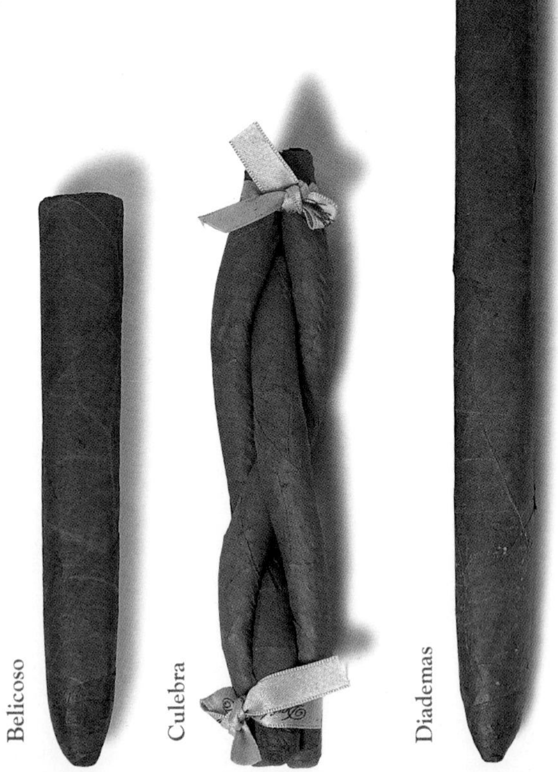

Belicoso

Culebra

Diademas

is usually shaped with a bulge in the middle. Perfectos can vary greatly in length, from 4 1/2 to 9 inches and can have a ring gauge between 38 and 48.

PYRAMID: A tapered-head cigar with an open foot (the end you light). These cigars are between 6 and 7 inches with a ring gauge of around 40 at the head that widens to between 52 and 54 at the foot. The difference between a pyramid and a torpedo is that the pyramid's foot is cut, whereas the torpedo has a closed foot.

Perfecto

Pyramid

JEFF HARRIS

Double Claro or Candela

Claro

Colorado Claro or Natural

Colorado

Colorado Maduro

Maduro

Oscuro

CIGAR BRANDS BY COUNTRY

The cigar brands below are grouped by country of origin. A heading such as "Honduras & Nicaragua" indicates that the same manufacturer makes the same brand in two different countries.

However, because of trademark disputes between the Cuban government and those who owned Cuban brands prior to Castro's revolution—and who have since established factories elsewhere—you will see some brand names listed twice, under Cuba and another country as well. These are *not* the same cigar. For example, note that the Cuban Hoyo de Monterrey has a strength designation of E (strong), while the Honduran Hoyo de Monterrey is designated C (medium).

The relative strength designations represent an average strength for each brand. There may be some variation among the different lines within each brand.

KEY: RELATIVE STRENGTH

A	Mild
B	Mild to Medium
C	Medium
D	Medium to Strong
E	Strong

BRAZIL
Canonero - A

CANARY ISLANDS
Don Xavier - C
Dunhill - C
La Regenta - B
Monte Canario - B
Penamil - C
Vargas - C/D

COSTA RICA
Bahia - B/C

CUBA
Bolivar - D
Cohiba - E
Cuaba - D
Diplomaticos - C
El Rey del Mundo - B/C
Fonseca - C
Gispert - B
H. Upmann - D
Hoyo de Monterrey - E
José L. Piedra - B
Juan Lopez - D
La Flor de Cano - C
La Gloria Cubana - D/E
Montecristo - C/D
Partagas - D/E
Por Larrañaga - B/C
Punch - E
Quai d'Orsay - C
Quintero - C
Rafael Gonzalez - D

Ramon Allones - D
Romeo y Julieta - D
Saint Luis Rey - D
Sancho Panza - D

DOMINICAN REPUBLIC

Arturo Fuente - D
Ashton - D
Avo - D
Avo XO - D
Bauza - D
Caballeros - C
Cabañas - C
Cacique - C
Canaria d'Oro - C
Carlos Toraño - C
Carrington - B
Casa Blanca - C
Cerdan - B
Cohiba - D
Credo - B/C
Cubita - C
Cuesta-Rey - C
Davidoff - D
Diamond Crown - D
Diana Silvius Diamond
   Vintage Selection - C
Don Diego - C
Don Leo - B
Don Marcos - B
Dunhill Aged 1989 - C/D
Dunhill Aged 1994 - C/D
El Sublimado - B
Fonseca - C/D
Fuente Fuente Opus X - E
H. Upmann - C
H. Upmann Chairman's
   Reserve - C
Hamiltons - C
Hamiltons Reserve - B
Henry Clay - C
Hugo Cassar - A
José Benito - C
José Martí - A

Juan Clemente - B
Knockando - B
La Aurora - C
La Corona - B
La Diva - A
La Flor Dominicana - B
La Habanera - B
La Unica - C
Leon Jimenes - C
Licenciados - D
Macabi - C/D
Match Play - B
Montecristo - D
Montecruz - C
Montero - B
Montesino - C
Moreno Maduro - B
Nat Sherman - C
Olor - B
Onyx - B
Oscar - C
Partagas - D
Paul Garmirian - D
Peter Stokkebye - B
Peterson - B
Playboy by Don Diego - C
Pleiades - C
Por Larrañaga - C
Primo del Rey - C
Private Stock Cigars - B
Ramon Allones - B
Rollers Choice - B
Romeo y Julieta - B
Royal Dominicana - B
Santa Damiana - C
Santa Maria - C
Savinelli Extremely Limited
   Reserve - C
Savinelli Oro - C
Siglo 21 - B
Sosa - C
Tabaquero - A
The Griffin's - C
Topper Centennial - B
Tresado - A

Troya - C
Vueltabajo - C

HONDURAS

Astral - C
Baccarat Havana
  Selection - C
Ballena Suprema - B
Bances - C
Belinda - C
Bering - B
C.A.O. - C
C.A.O. Gold - C
Camacho - C
Camórra - C
Carmen - n/a
Churchill - n/a
Cuba Aliados - D
Don Asa - B
Don Lino - B
Don Mateo - C
Don Melo - C
Don Pepe - B/C
Don Tomas - C
El Rey del Mundo - C/D
Encanto - C
Evelio - B
F.D. Grave - C
Felipe Gregorio - C
Gilberto Oliva - C
Gispert - B
H.A. Ladrillo - B
Habana Gold - B
Hoyo de Monterrey - C
Hoyo de Monterrey
  Excalibur - D
Hugo Cassar - A
La Diligencia - B
La Fontana - A
La Reserva - C
Las Cabrillas - C
Lempira - B
Maya - B
Mocha Supreme - B
Nat Sherman - C
Nestor 747 - C
Nestor 747 Vintage - C
Orient Express - C

Particulares - B
Petrus - C
Plasencia - C
Punch - C
Puros Indios - D
Saint Luis Rey - C
Sancho Panza - B
Santa Rosa - C
Tesoros de Copan - C
Thomas Hinds Honduran
  Selection - C
Topper - B
V Centennial - C/D
Virtuoso - C
Zino - C
Zino Connoisseur Series - C

HONDURAS & NICARAGUA

Padrón - C
Padrón 1964 Anniversary
  Series - C

INDONESIA

Celestino Vega - C

JAMAICA

Cifuentes by Partagas - C
8-9-8 Collection - B
Macanudo Vintage 1993 - B
Mario Palomino - B
Royal Jamaica - B
Temple Hall - C

JAMAICA & DOMINICAN REPUBLIC

Macanudo - B/C

MEXICO

Aromas de San Andres - B
Cruz Real - C
Excelsior - B
Hugo Cassar - A
Matacan - C
Ornelas - B
Santa Clara - C
Te-Amo - C
Te-Amo New York, NY - C

NICARAGUA

Al Capone - C/D
Don Juan - D
Habanica - C
Hugo Cassar - A
José L. Piedra - B
José Martí - B
Joya de Nicaragua - C
La Finca - D
Mi Cubano - C
Thomas Hinds Nicaraguan
  Selection - C

PANAMA

José Llopis - B

PHILIPPINES

Calixto Lopez - C
Double Happiness - C
Fighting Cock - C

Flor de Manila - B
La Flor de la Isabella - B
Tabacalera - A/B

U.S.A.

Don Tito - C
La Plata - B
La Tradicion - C
Signature Collection by
  Santiago Cabana - D

U.S.A. & DOMINICAN
REPUBLIC

Calle Ocho - C
El Rico Habano - C
Havana Classico - B
La Gloria Cubana - D/E
La Hoja Selecta - B

MARINA FAUST

ACCESSORIES

CUTTERS

There are many acceptable ways to cut a cigar, however, a double-edged guillotine cutter is perhaps the best way to prepare a cigar for smoking. Place the cigar firmly between the two blades, and clip the head off with a decisive stroke. The double-blade mechanism applies equal pressure to both sides of the cigar, providing the cleanest cut possible with very little damage to the cigar. It opens the entire head of the cigar, which allows for a smooth, even flow of smoke.

A single-blade guillotine achieves the same kind of open-ended cut. With a single blade, however, the cutting edge presses against only one side of the cigar and can distort its shape, sometimes rupturing or tearing the wrapper.

A scissors also creates an open-ended cut. Unless the scissors is sharp, perfectly balanced and appropriately sized for your hand, it is very hard to get the necessary leverage and stability needed for a clean cut. Also, a scissors is usually less portable than a guillotine cutter.

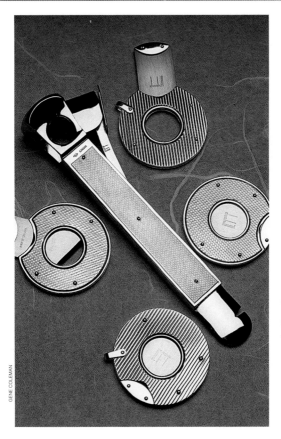

Another popular cutter is the wedge or V-cutter, which leaves a deep V-shaped gouge in the cigar. But if you chew your cigar, the wedge cutter may not be for you. As you moisten the cut edges of the V, they may collapse. Tars will accumulate in the now narrow opening, making the cigar taste harsh.

An auger, a drill or a piercer will punch a hole in one end of the cigar. However, this concentrates the smoke into a single aperture, where—as in a collapsed V-cut—tars may build up, creating a harsh smoke.

Using your teeth is acceptable if you don't have any other cutting device. Try to use the same principle as that of a double-edged guillotine—press your teeth against both sides of the cigar and bite firmly.

LIGHTERS

Once you cut the cigar, the next task is to light it. Regardless of the method you select, there are some basic rules. Never let the flame actually touch the cigar. Instead, rotate the cigar slightly above the flame tip so that you light the entire foot of the cigar. Blow through the cigar after embers appear on the end to expel any odors that may have come from the lighter or match.

Wooden matches remain one of the best ways to light a cigar. Always let the sulfur burn off before bringing the tip of the flame about 1/2 inch under the cigar's foot. A wide flame is best; don't hesitate to use two or three matches at once to get a proper light.

Small strips of cedar, called spills, are ideal for lighting cigars. But they can be inconvenient, as you must carry around little strips of wood as well as a lighter.

Butane lighters are perfectly acceptable. They burn with an even flame, and some lighters, made specifically for cigars, actually come with two burners to increase the size of the flame. The lighters often are windproof, and they are not only portable, but can be a beautiful piece of jewelry as well.

Some lighters are less than ideal. A fluid-fuel lighter must be used very carefully: If you pull the fumes through the cigar, they can affect the taste. But used properly, this type of lighter is perfectly functional.

Never light your cigar from a candle flame. The wax particles in the flame will ruin the taste of your cigar and make it burn less smoothly. And beware of anything other than wood that burns with a noticeable odor; the cigar could absorb these aromas, which would affect its taste.

HUMIDORS AND TRAVEL CASES

Cigars must be kept in a properly humidified environ-

ment. The correct ambiance is 70 to 72 percent relative humidity and a temperature of 70°F. A sealed environment is required to keep both elements stable. Avoid large or rapid fluctuations in either temperature or humidity; they can swell the bunch and crack the wrapper.

Diamond Crown

Wooden desktop humidors with humidity regulators are usually more than adequate to keep cigars. Built in sizes to accommodate anywhere from 50 to about 500 cigars, they offer a controlled environment. Check the cigars weekly, however, to ensure that the humidor maintains them at a proper moisture level. As for temperature, as long as you don't place the humidor next to a radiator, the cigars should be OK; most home environments remain between 68°F and 72°F.

Davidoff

J. C. Pendergast

Large standing cabinet humidors, with capacities of up to 1,500 cigars, are now available. They may include both temperature and humidity controls, and they have enough shelf space to store cigars in their original wooden boxes—an essential for the serious connoisseur. With some modifications, you can also outfit a closet with the proper humidification and temperature controls and ideally, with Spanish cedar shelving—to create a walk-in humidor.

A cigar carrying case is an important accessory; it protects the cigars you take with you when you go out. Be sure to select a size that will accommodate your favorite cigar. And you may want more than one style: a four- or

five-finger cigar holder is perfect for a day outdoors or a lengthy dinner party,

Daniel Marshall

while a two-finger model suffices for an after-dinner smoke with a friend—and fits in your pocket better.

Travel humidors are a separate category. They are built to hold anywhere from five to 25 cigars, and to fit easily in luggage or a briefcase. The humidification system will generally need recharging after two to five days of storage.

Elie Bleu

DRY CIGARS

You discover a box of your favorite cigars that you left in a closet for six months, and they're as dry as a bone. What do you do?

First, have patience. Put the cigars in a humidor that hasn't been charged in the previous week. Let them rest in the slightly dry humidor for a few days so the cigars absorb a little humidity. Then, partially fill the humidification device; let the cigars rest for another week before charging it fully. This process will prevent the cigars from getting too much humidity too soon. If you shock the cigars with too much moisture, they may burst (split the wrapper).

If you have a cabinet-style humidor, first place the cigars as far as possible from the humidification device. Move them closer to the humidification device little by little over a period of six weeks.

In any case, do not light up until the cigars are supple to the touch. A dry cigar will burn too hotly, and the flavor will seem burned or carbonized.

The same principle applies to cold cigars or ones that have been kept frozen. (There's nothing wrong with this storage method except that the cigars don't age.) You must allow the cigars to return to normal temperature slowly. If you light them too soon, the abrupt change in temperature may cause them to crack open or explode. Give chilled cigars at least two or three days at the proper temperature in a humidified environment before lighting up.

JEFF HARRIS

WHAT TO DRINK WITH YOUR CIGAR

Spirits and wine provide an ideal marriage with a premium hand-rolled cigar. Your choice of beverage depends on personal taste, and can vary according to the occasion. Sometimes what you want with your after-dinner cigar is the full-bodied, slightly sweet taste of a vintage Port; or maybe you want the palate-cleansing sharpness of an aged Cognac.

—PORT Port is a traditional partner for a great cigar. The sweetness and alcoholic power of vintage Port blend perfectly with a full-bodied smoke; even younger vintage Ports are appropriate because their strong tannins stand up to a spicy smoke. Nonvintage styles such as tawny Port also complement a cigar nicely because of the woody characteristics they acquire during long barrel aging.

—COGNAC The most popular traditional drink with fine cigars is Cognac or brandy. French Cognacs have solid cores of vanilla flavors derived from long years of oak-barrel aging. The crisp, clean flavors of the distilled wine keep the palate alive for the smooth, spicy flavors of a hand-rolled cigar. American brandies are often slightly fruitier, but display the same complex

COURTNEY GRANT WINSTON

flavors that come with barrel aging. Spanish brandies are usually deeper in color and often have a sweet, smoky component that enhances a cigar.

—BOURBON/SCOTCH/RUM Small batch and single barrel Bourbons, single malt Scotches and aged rums are superpremium products that have the complexity and depth of flavor to stand up to a cigar. The smoky quality of a fine single malt, derived from the smoked peat used to filter the spirit, marries perfectly with a cigar. Small batch Bourbons have a higher-than-standard proof level, which gives them a backbone of strong flavors; they complement medium- and full-bodied cigars. Kentucky straight Bourbons and Tennessee whiskey, although often a bit lighter, also mix well with cigars because of the charred wood flavorings that turn the liquors dark brown. Aged rums, with their slightly sweet profile and subtle burnt molasses flavors, can smooth out a cigar.

—WINE Complementary wines include Cabernet Sauvignon, both from California and Bordeaux, and Rhône varieties such as Syrah, Grenache and Mourvèdre. The latter have spicy flavors, including pepper.

Never light someone else's cigar; instead, offer your lighter or matches. The smoker usually draws in too hard to get a light quickly from someone else, and that can be bad for the cigar.

Don't puff too rapidly on a cigar. It will burn hot and acquire unsavory, burned flavors. A puff a minute is considered more than adequate to keep a cigar lit.

If you're in an area where your cigar smoke offends someone, put it out or move to another location if asked. If you're in an area that specifically allows cigar smoking, stand your ground; in this case, it's a management problem.

Don't play architect with the ash. If you wait too long to knock it off, it will end up on your pants or on the tablecloth. Watch for a small crack in the ash, then tap it off.

There are no rules for how far down to smoke a cigar. Some people smoke it only halfway. Others burn their fingers with a stub. Simply stop if the cigar starts to taste bad.

Never grind your cigar out in an ashtray. A cigar will self-extinguish quite rapidly. In fact, you'll release more odors into the air by grinding out your cigar than by leaving it alone.

In general, cigars with large ring gauges provide more flavorful, complex smokes. There's a simple reason: in a thick cigar, the blender can combine three or four different tobaccos to make the bunch. In a thinner ring gauge, it is extremely difficult to use more than two, or at most three, tobacco types.

CIGAR STORE ETIQUETTE

Shopping for cigars has become a full-time hobby
for some people. Cigar retailers are overloaded with
curious newcomers as well as demanding connoisseurs.
Here are some simple rules to keep in mind.

To test for moisture, cigars must be lightly grasped. But
if you squeeze them too hard, they will crack. Remember,
cigars wrappers are fragile; treat them that way.

Don't run an unpurchased cigar under your nose while
you take deep breaths. This practice is potentially
unsanitary, and smelling a cigar isn't going to tell a
layman a whole lot about it anyway.

Remember that retailers have many customers. Most
cigar shop owners are happy to provide information
and talk with people who walk in the door. But
don't be offended if they cut you off to deal with
someone else's questions. There's only so much time
in the day.

JONATHAN L. SMITH

GLOSSARY

BINDER—The portion of a tobacco leaf used to hold together the "bunch," the blend of filler leaves inside the cigar.

BLEND—The mixture of different types of tobacco in a cigar, including up to four types of filler leaves. Blending is an art, and blenders are responsible for brands keeping their signature taste from year to year.

BLOOM—A naturally occurring phenomenon in the cigar aging process, also called plume, caused by the oils which are exuded during later fermentations. It appears as a fine, white powder and can be brushed off. Not to be confused with cigar mold, which is bluish in color and stains the wrapper.

BOUQUET—The smell, or "nose," of a fine cigar. Badly-stored cigars lose their bouquet.

BOX—Cigar boxes come in all shapes and sizes. Traditional styles include:
* *cabinet selection:* wood boxes with a sliding top designed to hold 25 or 50 cigars.
* *8-9-8:* a round-sided box specifically designed to accommodate three rows of cigars—eight on top, nine in the middle, and eight on the bottom.
* *flat top, or 13-topper:* a flat, rectangular box with 13 cigars on top and 12 on the bottom, divided by a spacer.

BULK—A large pile of tobacco leaves in which fermentation occurs. See "Burros."

BUNCH—The mass of up to four different types of filler tobacco that are blended and held together by the binder to form the body of a cigar.

BUNDLE—A packaging method, designed with economy in mind, that uses a cellophane over-wrap. It usually contains 25 or 50 cigars, traditionally without bands. Seconds of premium brands are often sold in bundles.

CANDELA—A bright green shade of wrapper, achieved by a heat-curing process that fixes the chlorophyll content of wrapper leaves prior to fermentation. Also referred to as "double claro," or as American Market Selection (AMS.)

CAP—A circular piece of wrapper leaf placed at the head of a cigar to secure the wrapper. A good cut will leave part of the cap intact.

CAPA—The cigar's wrapper.

CHAVETA—An oval-shaped blade used by rollers in cigar factories to cut wrapper leaves.

CIGAR BAND—A ring of paper wrapped around the closed head of many cigars. Legend says that cigar bands were invented by Catherine the Great or by Spanish nobles to keep their gloves from being stained. Others credit their invention to a Dutchman named Gustave Bock, and state that the band helped keep the cigar wrapper together. Cigar bands are often printed with the name of the brand, country of origin, and/or indication that the cigar is hand-rolled. They also often have colorful graphics which have made them popular collectors' items. In many folk tales, a cigar band serves as a wedding band in impromptu ceremonies. For the record, it is equally appropriate to leave the band on while smoking a cigar or to remove it, as long as the cigar's wrapper leaf is not torn when the band is removed.

CLARO—A pale-green to light-brown shade of wrapper, characteristic of wrapper leaves grown in the shade.

COLORADO—A medium-brown to brownish-red shade of wrapper leaf

DOUBLE CLARO—
(see Candela)

DRAW—The amount of air that a smoker pulls through a lit cigar. A well-made cigar draws easily, yielding cool smoke. If the draw is too easy, the smoke will be too hot; if the cigar is plugged and the draw is tight, smoking it will not be relaxing.

FERMENTATION—Like fine wines, fine cigar tobaccos are the product of fermentation, and continue to go through additional stages of fermentation as they age. After the harvest, workers pile tobacco leaves into large "bulks," and moisten them to promote the primary fermentation. Temperatures inside a bulk may reach 140°F.

FIGURADO—A Spanish term that refers to cigars with exotic shapes, such as torpedos, pyramids, perfectos and culebras.

FILLER—The individual tobacco leaves used in the body of the cigar. A fine cigar usually contains between two and four different types of filler tobacco.

FLAG—An extension of the wrapper leaf shaped to finish the head of a cigar; used instead of a cap. Flags are sometimes tied off in a pigtail or a curly head. A flag is a good indication that a cigar was hand-made.

FOOT—The end of the cigar you light. In most types of cigars, it is pre-cut, but in torpedos and perfectos, it is sealed.

GRAN CORONA—A very big cigar; generally 9 1/4 inches by 47 ring gauge

GUM—A tasteless vegetable adhesive used to secure the wrapper leaf.

HABANO—A designation which, when inscribed on a cigar band, indicated that a cigar is Cuban. (Note: not all Cuban cigars are marked with "Habano" or "Havana.")

HAND—A sheaf of harvested tobacco leaves tied together at the top. Hands are piled together to make a bulk for fermentation.

HAND-MADE—A cigar made entirely by hand with high quality wrapper and long filler. All fine cigars are hand-made. Hand-rollers can generally use more delicate wrapper leaves than machines.

HAND-ROLLED—All hand-made cigars are hand-rolled, but some

"hand-rolled" cigars are machine made up to the point that the wrapper is hand-rolled.

HAVANA—1. The capital of Cuba, and the traditional center of manufacturing of Cuban cigars for export. 2. Cuban cigars are often called "Havanas." 3. "Havana" is also used as a term to describe tobacco types grown from Cuban seed in places such as the Dominican Republic, Honduras and Nicaragua.

HEAD—The closed end of the cigar; the end you cut before smoking.

HOT—A term used to describe a cigar that is underfilled and has a quick, loose draw. A hot cigar is likely to taste harsh, instead of mellow.

HUMIDOR—A room or box designed to maintain the proper humidity and temperature for cigar preservation and aging. Humidity should remain around 70%, and temperature should stay in the 65°F to 70°F range.

LIGERO—An aromatic tobacco which is one of the three basic types of filler tobacco. The name means "light" in Spanish. "Ligero" is also used to describe light wrapper leaves.

LONG FILLER—A term used to designate filler tobacco that runs the length of fine cigars. Machine-made cigars often use chopped filler.

MACHINE-MADE—Cigars made by machine use heavier-weight wrappers and binders and, in many cases, chopped filler, instead of long filler.

MADURO—A shade of wrapper varying from a very dark reddish-brown to almost black. The color results from longer exposure to the sun, a cooking process, or longer fermentation. The word means "ripe" in Spanish.

MOLD—1. A form used to shape the finished bunch for a cigar. It comes in two parts which are assembled and placed in a press. 2. A potentially damaging fungus that can form on cigars stored at too high a temperature.

OIL—Oil is the mark of a well-humidified cigar. Even well aged cigars secrete oil at 70-72% humidity, the level at which they should be stored.

OSCURO—A black shade of wrapper, darker than maduro, most often Brazilian or Mexican in origin.

"PERIOD OF SICKNESS"—A time when cigars should not be smoked. Fresh cigars are fine, as are aged ones; but avoid cigars between three months and a year old. (No reputable store would sell you a cigar of this age.)

PLUGGED—A description of a cigar that has a poor draw.

PURO—A Spanish term used to distinguish a cigar from a cigarette. Modern usage refers to a blend of tobaccos from one country.

RING GAUGE—A measurement of the diameter of a cigar, based on 64ths of an inch. A 40 ring gauge cigar is 40/64ths of an inch thick.

SECO—A type of filler tobacco which often contributes aroma and is usually medium-bodied. The word means "dry" in Spanish.

42

SHADE-GROWN—
Wrapper leaves that have been grown under a cheese cloth tent, called a tapado. The filtered sunlight creates a thinner, more elastic leaf.

SMOKING TIME—A 5-inch cigar with a 50 ring gauge, such as a robusto, should provide anywhere from 20 to 30 minutes of smoking pleasure. A double corona—a 7 1/2 inches—cigar with a 50 ring gauge—may give over an hour's worth of smoking time. A thinner cigar, such as a Lonsdale, smokes in less time than a cigar with a 50 ring gauge.

SUN-GROWN—
Tobacco grown in direct sunlight, which creates a thicker leaf with thicker veins.

"TOTALMENTE A MANO"—Made totally by hand, a description found on cigar boxes. A much better designation than "Hecho a Mano," (made by hand, which can be used for machine bunched filler that was finished by hand) or "Envuelto a Mano" (packed by hand.)

TUBOS—Cigars packed in individual wood, metal or glass tubes to keep them fresh.

TUNNELING—The unwelcome phenomenon of having your cigar burn unevenly. To prevent it, rotate your cigar now and then.

VINTAGE—When a vintage is used for a cigar, it refers to the year the tobacco was harvested, not the year the cigar was made.

VUELTA ABAJO—The valley in Cuba that many believe produces the best cigar tobacco in the world.

VOLADO—A type of filler tobacco, added for its burning qualities.

WRAPPER—A high-quality tobacco leaf wrapped around a finished bunch and binder. It is very elastic, and, at its best, unblemished.

THE MAGAZINE

W inner of the prestigious "Acres of Diamonds" award in 1997 for best consumer magazine launched in the past five years, CIGAR AFICIONADO began in September 1992 as a quarterly magazine and—because of its phenomenal success and great demand—in 1997 became a

bimonthly, publishing six issues per year. CIGAR AFICIONADO is an international success available in over 100 countries around the world. Paid circulation has grown to over 400,000, and total worldwide readership exceeds one million cigar lovers.

The magazine continues to hold true to its original mission: to provide cigar smokers with unparalleled, in-depth information about cigars. Since its inception, it has rated well over 1000 cigars. A panel of senior editors smokes the cigars "blind"—unidentified and unlabeled—and then rates them on a 100-point-scale. The panel has evaluated virtually every size of cigar and every brand that is available in the retail market.

CIGAR AFICIONADO has a commitment to present its readers with editorial excellence. There are no shortcuts in the creation of each issue. When you open CIGAR AFICIONADO, you know that you are holding the culmination of many hours of thought, planning and execution with only one standard in mind: giving you the best.

To Order Call
800-992-2442

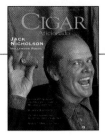

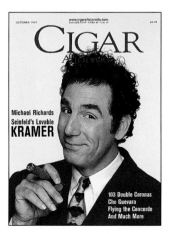

CIGAR INSIDER NEWSLETTER

Launched in January 1996, *Cigar Insider* is a monthly newsletter that provides useful and up-to-date information about cigars with a special emphasis on new products and new brands with cigar ratings. There are sections on cigar industry news, retail availability and prices—especially of Cuban cigars—in cities around the world, travel tips, upcoming cigar events and much more. The newsletter is available by subscription only.

CIGAR AFICIONADO'S BUYING GUIDE

This ultimate resource for cigar lovers provides a complete directory of cigars tasted in CIGAR AFICIONADO magazine, including rating, country of origin, type of tobacco used, and price, with descriptive notes on strength and flavor. It also has a comprehensive list of retail tobacconists in the U. S. and abroad who sell CIGAR AFICIONADO, and a worldwide guide to cigar-friendly restaurants.

SHANKEN'S CIGAR HANDBOOK

A Connoisseur's Guide to Smoking Pleasure—
From the editor and publisher of CIGAR AFICIONADO,

Marvin R. Shanken, comes a complete guide to the cigar-smoking experience. Shanken shows you how to navigate a market in which premium cigars are more and more in demand—and less and less available. With his guidance, you'll learn how to find a knowledgable tobacconist, how to identify, develop and expand your tastes, and how to select cigars you'll enjoy. You'll also learn the proper way to cut, light, hold, and smoke a cigar, important tips on cigar-store and smoking etiquette, and how best to store your cigars for long-term enjoyment. With an exhaustive list of cigar brands to help you identify your favorite smokes, a "Top 40" featured cigar section that includes room for your personal tasting notes, and a comprehensive glossary that will have you speaking the language of the aficionado in no time, *Shanken's Cigar Handbook* is the essential guide to beginning and maintaining a life-long pleasure.

CIGAR AFICIONADO'S WORLD OF CIGARS

Celebrate your love of fine cigars with the *World of*

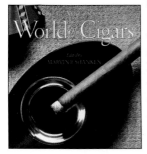

Cigars, an exquisite 135-page full-color collection of photographs and essays, edited by Marvin R. Shanken. The people, the places, the accessories and the collectibles—everything that makes the cigar such a unique cultural phenomenon—are brought together in this one fabulous collection.

47

CIGAR AFICIONADO'S APPOINTMENT DIARY

Plan your weeks in singular style with this distinctive desk calendar. The fourteen-month week-at-a-glance calendar incorporates witty quotes and insights from well-known cigar enthusiasts past and present, historical cigar trivia, and informative tips on cigar smoking. Beautiful photography and original line-art illustrations grace the pages. There is even space for your personal tasting notes,

JONATHAN SMITH

including a place to paste your favorite cigar bands. A ribbon marker is attached for easy reference.

CIGAR AFICIONADO ONLINE

The Internet home for cigar smokers around the world and the perfect complement to your copy of Cigar Aficionado. Search our vast database of cigar ratings, tasting notes, tobacconists and cigar-friendly restaurants. Interact live with our editors and industry experts. Peruse the back issue archive and read articles on art, celebrities, collectibles, gambling, sports and fashion. Research resorts and hotels around the world to help plan your next vacation. Access up-to-the-minute information such as professional and college sports scores and the stock prices of publicly traded cigar companies. Participate in our weekly poll and connect with other cigar lovers in chat forums. We invite you to visit Cigar Aficionado Online at **www.cigaraficionado.com.**

THE BIG SMOKE

The legendary Big Smoke offers the ultimate cigar experience. Cigar lovers have the opportunity to sample products from every major cigar manufacturer, and to look at or buy outstanding cigar accessories, from cutters and lighters to humidors. Representatives from leading producers of Scotch, Bourbon, vodka, rum, Port and Cognac pour their products and local restaurants provide food. Big Smokes are held in major cities across the United States. Check the calendar in Cigar Aficionado or visit our website at **www.cigaraficionado.com** for more information about a Big Smoke near you.

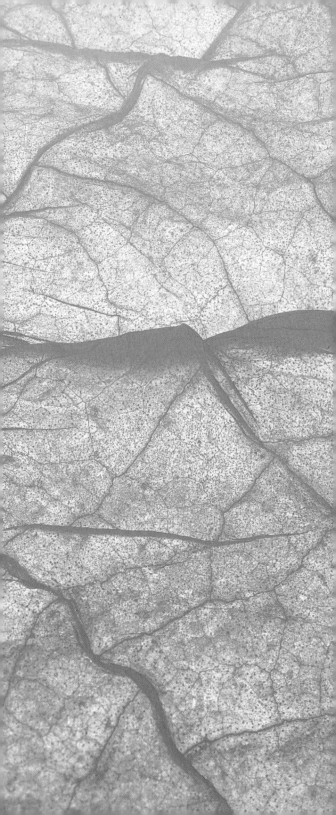